MW01178332

Addiction to Poetry

Trevor Muir

Addiction to Poetry
Copyright © 2019 by Trevor Muir

All rights reserved. No part of this publication
may be reproduced, distributed, or transmitted
in any form or by any means, including
photocopying, recording, or other electronic
or mechanical methods, without the prior
written permission of the author, except
in the case of brief quotations embodied
in critical reviews and certain other non-
commercial uses permitted by copyright law.

Tellwell Talent
www.tellwell.ca

ISBN
978-0-2288-1419-1 (Hardcover)
978-0-2288-1417-7 (Paperback)
978-0-2288-1418-4 (eBook)

This book is a compilation of all the poems I have written in my life. Each one comes from a very personal place within me. Some of the poems truly show me at my most fearful, sad, and lonely moments in my life, and others are examples of how I was feeling at a time when I was desperate and lost all hope.

Some are of love, hope, a general wonder or curiosity, and accomplishment, and others came from the experiences of people closest to me.

I have added a page that briefly describes where the inspiration for the poem(s) came from, to help better tell the story. For me, poems and writing became a personal outlet. They have given me a safe way to express my thoughts and feelings.

I hope you enjoy them. If they are at all relatable than that's even better. I hope that those who read these, and identify with them, will see that no matter how rough life may seem at any given time, it can get better if you just keep going.

Although the poems within these pages may be a bit random and unorganized, as is my life sometimes, they are raw and real. They are as I wrote them at that time.

I want to thank everyone who has taken the time to read any or all of them, and I hope you enjoy them as much as I am sure my Mom will. :) LOL

I am dedicating this book to my wife, Reni, my son, Jord, my dad, Roy, my mom, Joy, my two sisters, Denise and Ashley, my mother in law, Brenda, my sister in law, my brother in laws, and all my nephews and nieces. Each of you has given me love, inspiration, and support throughout my life. I certainly would not have been able to get through some dark days without you.

I also want to send a special thanks to all my friends, especially, Blaine, Lynda, Amanda, Martin and Colette. Each of you has not only encouraged me to write, but you have also helped me to find the courage to share my poems with others. I greatly appreciate you all.

I hope you all know how much I love you and how grateful I am to have you in my life.

Table of Contents

What is life?

I wrote this one after attending a couple funerals a few years ago. A minister at one funeral said, "What is life?" and than went into a bit of a sermon.

It got me thinking, and I woke up the next morning and jotted this down.

Hope you enjoy,

Trev

What is life?

Life is green grass and a hot sunny day.

It is puppies, and kittens and children at play.

It's friends and it's family.

It's handshakes and hugs.

It's the wind in your face and it's ladybugs.

It's a sunrise, a sunset, a bright starlit night.

It's saying I'm sorry right after a fight.

It's a rainbow, a blue sky, it's clouds and it's rain.

It is smiles and laughter, it's tears, and it's pain.

It's a loved one's last words and a baby's first breath.

Life is a beginning, and it is also death.

It is about mourning and about a long cry.

Life is about knowing and questioning why?

Life is a feeling that's never the same.

It is parents deciding on their newborn's name.

It's a child's excitement when it's Christmas eve.

It's saying goodbye, but not wanting to leave.

It's to win and to lose, it's to pass and to fail.

Life's the feeling inside when your dog wags its tail.

It's losing a loved one. It's sadness and grief.

It's about feeling nervous and feeling relief.

Life is about tripping and learning to fall.

It's about a best friend who is there when you call.

Life is confidence and it's uncertainty.

It's learning to become who you're meant to be.

Life's the stories that stay in an old coffee cup,

and it's, courage to try and to never give up.

It's hanging on tightly, but then letting go.

It is trust in your faith when you truly don't know.

Life is a gift from God up above.

And so, it must be that life surely is LOVE!!

I lie in bed beside you

I was watching my wife sleeping one evening. The room was lit up in such a beautiful way by the moonlight. I just watched her breathe in and out, and I felt so safe and grateful. I wrote this the next morning when I woke up.

Trev

I lie in bed beside you!

I lie in bed beside you and I look in your direction.

Through the window in our bedroom
I can see the moon's reflection.

It lights the room a little, so that I can see your face,

and it brings me to the present, to
a safe and special place.

I watch your chest rise and fall with
every breath you take,

and I try not to stir you, so I stay still for your sake.

In the quiet of the bedroom I watch you for a while.

In the presence of your beauty, I can't help but smile.

So, as I close my eyes to sleep, my
dreams will be all right.

'Cause you're the last thing that I
see, as I fall asleep tonight.

If my love for you could be measured

I wrote this for my wife on her birthday one year. It came to me while I was sitting in my truck so, I wrote it in her birthday card right before I gave it to her.

Trev

If my love for you could be measured

If my love could be measured in raindrops, then
my love it would flood the whole earth.

If my love could be measured in diamonds and
gold, then my love it would have endless worth.

If my love could be measured in miles,

then my love would go on endlessly.

If my love could be measured in sunlight,

then my love would be too bright to see.

If my love could be measured in time,
then forever would not compare.

Though my love for you cannot be measured,

in my heart you will always be there.

Goodbye Grandpa

The name of this one sort of gives it away. I had gone and visited my grandfather in the hospital when he was dying of cancer. I got to spend a few hours alone with him, visiting before I left town. I didn't say goodbye to him at the time. Instead I said I would come back and see him soon. When I told him, I would have to get going he held my hand said he loved me and started to cry. I quickly said I loved him and pulled away. Then I just left in a hurry. I didn't even stop to see my family on the way out. Just got in my car and drove. My Grandpa passed away a few nights later, and I never did get back to see him or talk to him again. I wrote this a few years back and read it out loud to let him know some of the things I wished I would have said and done when I was with him that day. I know that he knows I loved him though, so I have peace in that.

Trev

Goodbye Grandpa

You held me as a baby, I brought you lots of pleasure.

You loved me more than life itself.

To you I was a treasure.

You watched me grow into a man.

Had faith in all I'd do.

Though I never really told you,

I wished I'd be like you.

Though I didn't visit often, you
were in my heart all days

And it took 'til you were dying to
see the error of my ways.

I'm so grateful for the time we had before the very end.

Because I got to hold your hand,
my broken heart will mend.

I still need to tell you some things, and
I hope you'll hear my words.

I'll send them to the angels on the
wings of pure white birds.

I'm sorry that I ran away the day that you were dying.

I couldn't stand there any longer when
I saw that you were crying.

I told you that I loved you, but I was
just too scared to show it.

And now that you're in heaven, I
pray to God you know it.

The past 20 years went by so fast I didn't stop to see,

That you were getting older and
how precious time can be!

And now that you have passed away,
I miss you many days.

And I wish that I could turn back time
and change my selfish ways.

You were more than just a Grandpa.

You were a mentor and a friend.

And you always loved me dearly,
right up to the very end.

Now I haven't said goodbye, so I have too set you free.

But there's one more thing I have
to say before I let you be.

I'm sorry that I ran away the day that you were dying.

Because if I'd have stood there longer,

You would have seen me crying.

Fall

Driving home from Northern Alberta one day I was overwhelmed with the amazing colors and beautiful changes that come with fall. As I drove this popped into my head, so I jotted it down when I got home.

Trev

Fall

The tree leaves wear their colored coats,
And songbirds sing their farewell notes.
The squirrels stash and geese migrate,
And bears prepare to hibernate.
When summer's gone and winter's near,
The autumn air is crisp and clear,
And grass will glisten at first light.
When Jack Frost visits in the night.

The vegetation all decays,
To grow again with spring's sunrays.
And poplars start to shed their leaves
with just the slightest of a breeze.

The animals will thicken fur,
instinctively, this is for sure.

I gaze in awe and great delight, with
all the colors in my sight.
From Mother Nature to us all,
A gift from God.
We call it fall!

My heart skipped a beat

I wrote this poem for a friend who liked a girl he had
noticed a few times at an establishment he liked to visit.
He was afraid to go speak to her, so I wrote this for him
as an icebreaker.

Trev

My heart skipped a beat

I saw you standing across the room,
and my heart skipped a beat.

Your beauty made my legs so weak I
could barely move my feet.

I managed to get closer, so that I could see your eyes,

And they let me see right to your
heart and see it held no lies.

I watched you for a little bit… no, actually for a while.

And I saw how your eyes sparkle, every time you smile.

So, I have too tell you something, in
case again we never meet.

The moment that I saw your face…
my heart did skip a beat.

Promise to my baby

I wrote the one below along time ago. We had just bought a new house, and in what became our workout room, there was a very small handprint on one of the walls. It wasn't very noticeable, but I saw it while running on the treadmill one day. Anyway... this is what came to me.

Trev

Promise to my baby

I see your tiny fingers, and I see your little toes.

Your eyes are shut so tightly, but I see your little nose.

I see your little arms and hands, your little legs and feet.

I cannot see your heart, but I can feel it beat.

I see your little ears and lips, the
sparse hair on your head.

I cannot see your love, but I can feel it instead.

I watch you little baby, 'cause you're very special, see?

You're a perfect little package that God has gifted me.

So I promise I will nurture you and give you all my love,

And I'll care for you on earth for our Father up above.

The killing ground

This is one of the first poems I can remember writing. I wrote it as a grade nine class assignment for a Remembrance Day contest. My teacher entered it into a local competition. She encouraged me to write more, but it would be decades later before I wrote poems again.

Trev

The killing ground

I looked around the killing ground,

That lonely desolate place.

Where people live and people die.

You can see the horror on each face.

My friend and I, we used to laugh about that crazy war,

But now we're here and life is special.

It makes me want to cry.

The thought of war it scares me so,

The thought that I might die.

I turn to run, but think again as I
hear that dreadful shot.

I turn around and ask myself,

Am I dead or not?

I look to the ground and see my friend,

His body lying still.

From that day on I've asked myself,

Was it worth the pain?

To see my best friend, die in war.

And I ask myself again!

When you look into a mirror

This was a bit random. I was reflecting on a time in my life when I couldn't bear to look at my own reflection. I just had such low self-esteem. I was full of fear and shame, and guilt had become my norm. I did some things to change my life and overcome those feelings, and one day I realized I was looking into my own eyes in the mirror without the negative emotions I had felt most of my life. This prompted me to write the poem.

Trev

When you look into a mirror

When you look into a mirror, do you see your face?

Or has someone unfamiliar seemed to take its place?

Can you look the person in the
mirror directly in the eyes?

Or do you have to look away because
they know your lies?

Does the person in the mirror look
at you with disrespect?

Is there shame and sadness in their
face that you seem to detect?

Do you ever turn the lights off when
you're looking in the mirror?

With the hope that when they're on
again, the face will disappear?

Do you ever fear the morning most and feel quite
insane, because the person in the mirror

wants to haunt you once again?

If you look into a mirror and do not see
your face, because someone unfamiliar

has seemed to take its place,

Just stare at the reflection, and say I'm proud of you,

And I'll always love you very much,
no matter what you do!

Say this every morning and every afternoon,

Then the face that's unfamiliar
will disappear quite soon.

Just focus on becoming who you really want
to be, and the face that's in the mirror

will be the one you want to see.

Our Love

Sitting on the couch near my wife one day I was thinking about what our love was like. For some reason these words came to me, so I grabbed a paper and wrote this poem.

Trev

Our Love

When we sit in silence, I can hear you.

When we almost touch, I can feel you.

When I close my eyes, I can see you.

And every time my heart beats,

It beats for you

This is our Love!

What is Love?

I saw a sign while walking that simply said... what is love?
Anyway, it got me thinking and this is what I wrote.

Trev

What is Love?

Is love the twinkle in an eye, a gentle
laugh, a soft sweet sigh?

Is love the flutter of a heart, or a
feeling when you are apart?

Is love the whisper in an ear, or
kindness that is most sincere?

Is love the feeling in a touch, or those
moments that you miss so much?

Is love like dancing in the rain, or is it joy, or is it pain?

Is love faith, mixed with fear, or is
love a longing to be near?

Is love just like a shining star that
feels so close although it's far?

Is love like heat straight from the
sun, or is it passion, is it fun?

Is love a feeling in the air, or is it in a gazing stare?

Is love crazy, is it blind, is love the
rarest thing you'll find?

Is love a laugh, is love a tear, is it the
thing you'll hold most dear?

Is love compassion, a warm embrace,
is it a glow on someone's face?

Is love like words an angel sings,
carried on an eagle's wings?

Is love a cuddle, a hug or kiss?

Is love all or none of this?

Grandma's poem

This was a poem I wrote for my Grandma on her birthday. It sums up many of our family's, collective feelings and experiences with her.

Trev

Grandma

You are just the right amount of strength,
when the family feels weak.

You are just enough compassion when
compassion's what we seek.

You give us all some guidance, in
your silent, special way.

And you live your life with faith in
God each and every day.

You have baked us lots of cookies and
we've skunked you in crib games.

We've all heard you "Tsk, tsk!" grandpa
and you have misspelled our names.

You have opened up your home to us,
been there for us through our pain.

You've shown us through thick and
thin your love does never wane.

We don't visit quite as often as we
should, although I'll say,

You are loved by every one of us,
each minute of each day.

You have raised all of your children;
you're a grandma, been a wife,

You're a sister and a friend.

Well you're living quite a life!

You are such an inspiration.

You mean more than words can say.

So, we wish you every gift from God, on this special day.

If a wind could carry love

Here is a poem that came to me when I was in line for the log ride with my family at Calaway park a few years back. The wind was blowing, and I just felt a lot of love for my family.

Trev

If a wind could carry love

If a wind could carry love, I'd send my love to you.

I'd send it on a breeze that very gently blew.

I'd send the breeze through meadows,

Where the flowers bloom each spring,

And I'd send the breeze through heavens,

Where the angels come to sing.

I'd ask the sun to kiss it, so its warmth

would be just right.

Then I'd ask the stars to sparkle bright

and fill it with their light.

I'd pray that God would bless it, then

I'd pray to God you knew

That if a wind could carry love,

I'd send my breeze to you.

Oh my little boy

I was working through some difficult moments in my life and as part of the process I was asked to forgive myself and let go of some of the pain and burden I was carrying.

For some reason, I chose to let it go by writing this poem.

Trev

Oh my little boy

Oh, my little boy, don't cry anymore.

You no longer have too be sad, or let your heart be sore

You always were so precious and
one day I hope you'll see,

That although you were not perfect, you
were the best that you could be.

You have carried all my sadness for so many days,

And I'm sorry that I burdened you in so many ways.

Now I've shared my tears and sorrow,

And I've shared my fears and pain.

I have asked God to remove them,

So, you won't carry them again.

You no longer need to stay with me
to help me to be strong.

So, I ask, please go and play now,
before your time is gone.

I'll love you for eternity, but it's goodbye now you see.

You are no longer to stay

The little boy inside of me!

I am!

I was out for a jog one day and was thinking about the universe, God, and how everything is connected. This popped into my head, so I came home and wrote it down.

Trev

I am!

I am the air, a plant, a bird.

I'm every noise that's still unheard.

I am the wind, a gentle breeze.

I'm everything a human, sees.

I'm the sparkle in a newborn's eye.

I'm also in a baby's cry.

I am laughter; I am a tear.

I'm all the sounds that you can hear.

I am darkness, and I'm light.

I am a butterfly in flight.

I am a mouse, a raging bull.

In fact, I'm every animal.

I am space, and I am earth.

I'm part of death and I am birth.

I am compassion and eternal love.

I'm all the galaxies above.

I'm all creation old and new.

I'm everything including you!

I lie awake in darkness

This one is very personal to me. I wrote it during those days when I was so lost. Although I could logically see how good my life was, I didn't feel it. Instead I was very lonely, sad, confused and, truthfully, full of fear.

I haven't shared my poems with many people, especially this one, but I wanted to include it. I'm not sure how many people will relate to it, but someday someone might be feeling this way. If so, please know that I felt this way too, and came through to the other side. Anyway, I feel like this one is a step toward opening myself up...

Trev

I lie awake in darkness

I lie awake in darkness, but there's
bright light all around me.

My visions nearly perfect, but I can barely see.

My mind's not calm and steady, it races on and on.

Sometimes I think that it won't stop
until my sanity is gone.

The noise that echoes in my ears hasn't any sound,

And just adds to my confusion as my
world goes around and round.

I pray that there's a heaven, though
sometimes it's hard to tell.

There are times in my life when I
know that there's a hell.

These are moments when there's
agony in every single breath.

These are moments I'm afraid of life,
but more afraid of death.

How life was when I drank

I used to have drinking dreams that felt so real, whoa...! I wrote this after one of those experiences.

Trev

How life was when I drank

Its been a few days since I've had my last drink.

About fifty-two and a half days, I think.

Last night before bed I felt very sane, but when
sleeping I dreamt' I was drinking again.

I sat in a lounge and I drank lots of beers and
though I was dreaming, I felt my old fears.

I felt very frightened and lonely inside, and I
felt shame and guilt that I wanted to hide.

I was panicked and sweating when I woke
up, and I looked round the room

for an empty beer cup,

But my wife was asleep; she was near my right hand.

To the left was my Big Book sitting on the nightstand.

So, I crept out the room and I kneeled to pray,

Cause these words to God I needed to say.

Thank you, God for giving me life, and
thanks for the gifts of a son and a wife.

And thanks for the courage you give me each day.

And I'm grateful you guided me into AA.

And thanks for the dream, it helped me see clear

Of how bad life could be if I drank one more beer.

As I prayed for his guidance, I felt relief then.

I opened my eyes and I just said, "Amen."

As I went back to bed, I had no more fear,

And I chose that tomorrow, I would not drink a beer.

And as I fell asleep, I had God to thank,

That I hadn't forgotten how life was when I drank.

I am simply powerless

The poem I'm about to share is very personal to me and I guard it closely.

It truly tells my story of some personal struggles. I hope that anyone who identifies with this poem will find some hope in it.

I am simply powerless!

The shame, the guilt, the deep regret,
the never-ending fear.
The cycle starts all over as I pick up that first beer.
I fight the urge with all my will,
but always it's in vain,
'Cause I know the day will come
when I take a drink again.
I try a different tactic, a new strategy to quit.
I walk and run for miles; I can stop if I get fit!
I'll try and count my drinks, no wait!
Knowledge is the key!
Or I'll only drink red wine,
Then I won't get drunk
you'll see.
I will take up a religion or I'll finally take that trip,
Or the next time that I do drink,
I won't gulp it, I'll just sip.
I'll pray when I'm hung over and I'll promise to my wife
That I'll never drink again,
That should surely ease her strife.

I try to quit and try again; each time ends in defeat.

My addictions getting stronger; I'm
not sure it can be beat.

My family does not understand, the truth is nor do I.

Why don't I just stop drinking, if
I know that I might die?

I'm living almost every day in agony and pain.

My mind it races on and on; I surely am, insane!

I am lonely when I'm all alone and

I'm lonely in a crowd,

And I'm thinking that I'm crazy,

'Cause my thinking's very loud.

I know I don't know how to live.

I'm afraid with every breath,

That each time I take another drink
I'm closing in on death.

My life is a disaster!

I'm up against the wall!

I am taking my last beating from this foe called alcohol.

I am finally on my knees.

I'll accept my life's a mess,

And when it comes to alcohol,

I'm simply Powerless.

I was lying on the bathroom floor

I believe this poem tells the story on its own. The inspiration came from personal experiences, and a time a friend shared her similar experiences.

Trev

I was lying on the bathroom floor

I was lying on the bathroom floor shaking like a leaf.

I had never felt such loneliness,
such sadness or such grief.

I was wet cause I was sweating; I
was cold, and I was hot.

My head was pounding badly, and
my stomach hurt a lot.

I could not recall the evening, and
my mind raced on and on.

And despair and fear were setting in,
cause my memory was gone.

My body pain was torture; I could not get off the floor.

But the mental pain and agony that
tortured me much more.

I could not believe it happened. I
had gotten drunk again!

And the thoughts that I was thinking
made me sure I was insane.

I thought about my options and one of them was death.

I might have truly welcomed it, as
I suffered every breath.

I closed my eyes to try and sleep,
but my body jerked a lot,

And the fear that I might truly die
consumed my every thought.

I could not imagine living but was too afraid of death.

Then fear consumed my mind again,
this might be my last breath.

I was alone and I felt frightened, and
I could see what I became.

When hopes and dreams I'd once had,
were replaced by guilt and shame.

I thought about a lounge, a drink to take my pain away,

But this day I made a different choice,

I made the choice to pray.

Now I look back on my life without
remorse, without regret.

I no longer fear the past, nor fear
what hasn't happened yet.

And I'm sure that I'm alive today,
because God heard my voice,

on that day I thought I'd take a drink
but made a different choice.

All the things I lost

Pretty much sums up my journey through a program for sober living.

Trev

All the things I lost

I was really, quite amazed when I took the time to think.

About all the things I lost, because I took a drink.

I sometimes lost my wallet, and at times I lost my keys.

I often lost my balance. (Then I'd
scrape my hands and knees.)

I lost a lot of shoes and belts; one time I lost my car.

But thankfully I found it parked outside a different bar.

I lost a lot of money and I lost my dignity.

I lost my sense of right from wrong
and my self respect you see.

I lost some of my friends and I nearly lost my wife.

I surely lost my sanity,

When I prayed "God take my life!"

I had lost a lot of things when I
came through an AA door,

But little did I know I was about to lose some more.

I slowly lost my shame and guilt for all the things I did,

And I lost some deep resentments
that I had gotten as a kid.

I lost some insecurity, and the need to overthink.

And as I worked the program, I
soon lost the urge to drink.

I lost reliance on self will and slowly lost some fears,

And as I opened up a bit, I lost a lot of tears.

I lost some of my selfishness, much
sadness and much grief.

And I lost a lot of anger, and then I truly felt relief.

I lost some of my ego and I lost some foolish pride.

And I lost the pain and hurt that I
had stuffed deep down inside.

I lost some selfish pity and the thought I want to die.

And I lost the crazy notion that it's not ok to cry.

I lost my lack of feelings, my inability to love.

And I lost my lack of faith and trust in a God above.

I lost some desperation and the loneliness within.

And I lost my urge to fight and
learned surrender's how I win.

Now my life today's amazing, and
though it did come at a cost,

I'm grateful to my God today for all the things I lost.

Grew up in my nest!

A very close friend of mine asked if I would write a poem for her. Her mother had recently passed away, and she had given her daughter a picture of three blue birds in a nest. Her mother had said that those birds represented her children. Lynda, Julie and Joe. It took me a long time to get any connection with the picture, but one night, months after Lynda had asked if I would write something, these words came to me. I hope you enjoy it.

Trev

Grew up in my nest!

To Lynda, Joe and Julie,

All three of you were born to me,
a gift from God above.
Each one unique, but just the same
he filled you with his love.

Through all the ups and downs we faced while living in
our nest,
When God placed you together, then
I knew that you'd been blessed.

Through you he taught me patience, though it didn't
always show.
He taught me love and tolerance, as
I watched you slowly grow.

He filled me with excitement, the first time that you
each walked,
And he covered me in goose bumps,
the first time you each talked.

Through you I learned I'd make mistakes; there is much
I didn't know.
Though it didn't come that easily,
I learned I must let go.

I learned I'd live through sleepless nights, through
worry and through fears.

And I learned you'd live through broken
bones, through bruises, scrapes and tears.

I watched you bond together, and at times I watched
you fight.
And I learned you'd go to any lengths
to prove that you were right.

I watched you live through broken hearts, through
sadness and through pain,
and I watched you love each other,
while you learned to love again.

I watched you all go separate ways, but
never grow apart, and I know you hold a
special place within each other's hearts.

You will always be a family, be together 'til the end,
because you're more than just three
siblings, to each other you're a friend.

As I watch you all from heaven now, I truly am at rest,
and I love you all my little ones,
Who grew up in my nest.

Where is Gods Love?

I was struggling with the idea of spirituality, faith and God. I kept noticing that I could see something special in babies, that seemed to be a divine sparkle or feeling of joy and love. One day I wrote this. Hope you get something from it.

Trev

Where is God's Love?

You ask me where God's love is.

Well it's in a baby's eyes.

It's also in a baby's laugh and in a baby's cries.

You ask me where God's love is.

Well, it's in a baby's fingers.

And when the baby's fast asleep,
his love is there; it lingers.

You ask me where God's love is.

Well it's in a baby's hair.

It's in a baby's smile and in a baby's breath of air.

You ask me where God's love is.

Well it's in a baby's toes.

It's in a baby's ears and in a baby's nose.

You ask me where God's love is.

Well it's in a baby's chin.

It's in a baby's arms and legs, and in a baby's skin.

You ask me where God's love is.

Well it's in a baby's heart.

His love is very strong in there.

It's in there from the start.

You ask me where God's love is.

Well it's in a baby's soul.

His love is deep inside there and
helps make the baby whole.

You ask me where God's love is.

Well it's certainly in you.

Because if I'm not mistaken, weren't
you once a baby too?

God's Gift

It has taken me years to get here, but I believe we have all been given the gift of life, which means we have been given the gift of time. There is nothing more perfect than the exact moment we're in. Each second will never be repeated, and no experience will ever be precisely the same. What's great about this is no matter how dark or sad it is in this moment, it can and will be different. All pains can be replaced with, hope, peace and love. I certainly do not try and sell people on God, spirituality or faith, but this came into my head when I was running in Kelowna one day many years ago. It hit me that life is really millions, or billions of tiny moments and that God's gift is the present. I came from a very dark place in my life to a place where I feel alive, ok, peaceful at times, and mostly content and happy. Today I know its ok to feel sadness and pain because those too will pass.

As some of my poems indicate I was living in a hell inside my head. Today I'm grateful for my life and for the people in it. As I have mentioned these are very personal to me and come from a special place in my heart and soul. I hope you not only enjoy them but that they help in some small way.

Trev

GOD'S GIFT

Look back fondly, but momentarily on
memories, as this is the past.

Look ahead with hope, faith and courage
momentarily as this is the future.

Be present right now.

As this is GOD'S GIFT.

Live in this moment with honesty and integrity.

Look at the world through a child's eyes,

With openness and wonder!

Feel reborn each day, each hour, each minute.

As two moments will never again be the same.

Open your heart to Love.

And your soul to God.

Then find inner peace.

Then live life, right now, this moment.

Because this is the present.

And this is GOD'S GIFT!

Our little baby boy

I wrote this one for some good friends of ours. Their daughter, who is super close to us, had a very premature baby. He only lived for hours. She was in the hospital in Edmonton, and she had her Mom call my wife and I to ask if we would come and see her son before they let him go. I held the little guys hand for a few minutes, and we were able to be there for her, and their family. I wrote this poem that eve.

Trev

Our little baby boy

Your time with us was way too short, our little baby boy.

And though you weren't here very long,
you brought us so much joy.

Although our hearts are broken when
we think of you, we'll smile,

Cause though God called you home too
soon, you were ours for awhile.

You'll never be forgotten son. Our
love with you we'll send.

Cause you're no longer suffering, our
broken hearts will mend.

It's time to say our last goodbye, so go in peace; be free.

But in our hearts, you will live on for all eternity.

Though I never got to rock you

A dear friend of mine asked me one day if I could write a poem for someone close to her. The young lady had lost her baby pre-birth and she wondered if I would write a poem for her. This one took a long time to come together. The words finally did come to me in the middle of a night, so I got up and wrote it.

Trev

Though I never got to rock you!

Though I never got to rock you or tuck you in at night.

Though I never got to snuggle you,
or hold you, oh so tight.

Though I never got to know you,

One day I'll think of you and smile.

Cause though God called you home so soon,

You were mine for a while.

I never got to show you just how much I love you, so

Now that you're in heaven, I pray to God you know.

So, I'll send my love up to you, and I'll send it in a kiss.

I'll pass it through an angel's lips,

So, I know that it won't miss.

Someday I'm sure I'll see you as a twinkle in my eye.

Or as a bright and shining star, in a starlit sky.

I'll truly miss you, always.

I can't hide that or pretend.

But in time my pain will dissipate,
my broken heart will mend.

Now that you are safe in heaven, I have too set you free.

But before I say goodbye, know in
my heart you'll always be!

Even when we must say goodbye

I wrote this after my father-in-law, Daryl, passed away. That was a few years ago now. It came from what I believed would be his perspective and I really do believe that love doesn't have to end after someone passes. I shared it back than with my wife and Mother in law and now with each of you. I hope you enjoy.

Trev

Even when we must say goodbye

So many years have gone by now.

Don't look back at time that we've lost.

I'd do it all over with you again,
no matter what the cost.

Our friendship has weathered the storm.

Our true love has saved us some days.

The dark clouds have drifted away now, and
our hearts feel the warmth of sunrays.

We have cried tears of joy and of sorrow.

We've looked good times and bad in the eye.

You have been my best friend and I love you,

But our paths now have come to a Y.

So, move on your journey alone now,

As tough as it is you must try,

A new life is awaiting your entry

But now it is my time to die.

So please keep on living life fully,

And remember the love that we share.

But please open your heart to another,

As I've already had my time there.

I can leave now with peace in my body,

And I'll watch you from heaven above.
There's no reason for sadness or heartbreak
Cause I now know that I've felt true love.
There's no reason for sadness or heartache,
Just remember our love... please don't cry.
Cause our love does not have to end,
Even when we must say goodbye!

Inspiration for Haikus

I wrote these at a class I attended. We picked 6 words from a bag and had two use them to write 2 Haikus. My words were: wings, soaring, souls, as well as river, stone and mother.

Trev

Haikus

I'm an eagle's wings.
Soaring I make the winds sing.
Souls to God I bring.

River flows in me.
I'm stone eroding to sand.
Feeding the mother land.

If humans were all color blind

I had been really thinking a lot about our world. I believe in the goodness of people in general. However, it always amazes me that there is still such prejudice at times. While I was pondering, this poem popped into my head, so I wrote it down.

Trev

If humans were all color blind

If humans were all color blind, would
people truly be more kind?

Or if there was no race or creed,

Would there be less angst and greed?

If we all wore the same colored skin,

Would we be judged from within?

Would we see differently through our eyes,

If we all wore the same disguise?

Would wars decline or violence end?

Would peace on earth be the new trend?

Would hatred end and love survive?

Would more compassion come alive?

And who'd be slaves and who'd be free

If color was not there to see?

The world could be a better place

I'd like to think... although,

Because we aren't all color blind,
I guess we'll never know.

Kilimanjaro poem

I had some inspiration on our plane ride home from Africa. It kind of summarizes the climb up Kili, that Marty and I did together.

Trev

Kili

We climbed up many boulders, and we
hiked through clouds and rain.

Then we'd see blue skies and sunshine,
then the clouds would come again.

At times the wind would blow so hard,
at times we'd want to stop.

But that was not an option on our journey to the top.

We smiled when we saw the
peak... good God it was so far!

And we looked up in amazement as
the sky shared its first star.

Sometimes we'd walk in silence and
at times we'd talk a lot.

We'd tell stories of our childhood, of
some things so long forgot.

We'd laugh about the bathrooms. It
seemed better than to cry.

And we'd stand amazed in awe at
the mountain in the sky.

We saw all God's creations, saw the beauty and the light.

Then we'd hunker down in darkness
'til the stars came out at night.

We'd laugh through tired muscles and
we'd push through aches and pain.

Then we'd sleep in cold and dampness
and get up and go again.

At times we felt excited and at times we felt so drained.

And at times we were insane, but
neither one of us complained.

At times we prayed in silence, and
at times we prayed out loud.

Then we'd feel God around us as we
climbed right through a cloud.

We shared about our lives and we
shared our dreams and fears.

And moments from the peak, we also shared some tears.

The mountain asked for courage, determination, pride,

But it gave us peace, serenity, and
contentment deep inside.

The mountain took some sadness and
replaced the void with love,

As we gazed into a bright blue sky,
watching eagles soar above.

Then we climbed a ladder to the sky,
in the darkness of the night,

And our hearts were filled with gratitude
at the dawn of morning light.

It truly asked for everything, but
it gave us so much more,

As we stood upon its peak, a few
steps from heaven's door.

So we bowed down to this mountain
'cause it made our bodies whole,

And gave thanks to God and Kili...
for filling up our soul.

Someday too, today

Hope you all can get something from this one. I wrote this after the funeral of a friend where my buddy, Harvey, who was giving the eulogy, spoke about all the "some days" that we never do. This was also very shortly after an experience when I gave one of my very best friend's CPR in Princess Island Park: long story. Anyway, I had a lot of emotions going on and was really considering life. This is what came to me.

Trev

Someday too, today

Someday I'll climb a mountain;
someday I'll ride a horse.

Someday I'll take that lesson, or
I'll finish off that course.

Someday I'll learn to fly a plane;
someday I'll ride my bike.

Someday I'll sleep beneath the stars
and go on that long hike.

Someday I'll run that marathon;
someday I'll learn to cook.

Someday I'm going to lose some weight
and read my favorite book.

Someday I'm going to work less and
someday I'll take a trip.

Someday I'll spend more time with
friends and I'll sail on a ship.

Someday I'll show more empathy to everyone I meet.

Someday I'll show more kindness
to a stranger on the street.

Someday I'll volunteer my time,
give more to those in need.

Someday I'll grow a garden and
I'll hand plant every seed.

Someday I'll be more patient with
my child and my wife.

Someday I'll cherish moments, as
they happen in my life.

Someday I'll act more childlike;
someday I'll laugh much more.

Someday I'm going to love like I have never loved before.

Someday I'll play more with my kids,
spend more time with my wife.

Someday I'll find more balance in my very crazy life.

Someday I'm going to do the things
I've never done before.

Someday I'm going to take some risks,
walk through an unknown door.

Someday I'm going to let all my emotions run awry.

Someday I will allow myself to just be sad and cry.

Someday I will be happier; I'll feel more inside.

Someday I'll watch a full moon as
it shifts the ocean's tide.

Someday I'm going to worry less
and focus less on wealth.

Someday I'm going to have more fun
and focus more on health.

Someday I'll tell my parents what
they truly mean to me.

Someday I'll be the person that I truly want to be.

Someday I'll tell my siblings that I love them very much.

Someday I'll hug my family more
and treasure every touch.

Someday I'll watch the sun rise and
I'll watch as the sun sets.

Someday I'll forgive others and let go of my regrets.

Someday I'll be more present; I'll
be more aware each day.

Someday I'll gain more faith and
I'll take more time to pray.

Someday I'll have no some-day's
left, as someday I will die.

So, change your some-day's to today,
before they all pass by.

About the Author

Trevor Muir grew up in Elmworth, a small farming community in Northern Alberta. He learned at an early age the importance of family, friends, and community. He also learned that working hard and being kind were essential to getting ahead but giving back to others was truly what life was about. His life has led him down many paths that he could have never imagined, and he has had the opportunity to meet some of the most amazing people on the planet.

He strongly believes in sharing experiences in the hopes that it will help others to see they are not alone, and inspire them to become the best version of themselves.

Trev